This book belongs to

work it i
end supp

You can Do Great Things

Michele Steinhauser

illustrated by Yudthana Pongmee

A Faith Parenting Guide
is found on the last page of this book.

Faith Kids™ is an imprint of
Cook Communications Ministries, Colorado Springs, CO 80918
Cook Communications, Paris, Ontario
Kingsway Communications, Eastbourne, England

YOU CAN DO GREAT THINGS
© 2000 by Michele Steinhauser for text and Yudthana Pongmee for illustrations.

Scripture marked (NASB) is taken from the *New American Standard Bible*,
© the Lockman Foundation 1960, 1962, 1963, 1968, 1971, 1972, 1973, 1975, 1977.

Scripture marked (NIV) is taken from the *Holy Bible: New International Version* ®.
Copyright © 1973, 1978, 1984 by International Bible Society. Used by permission
of Zondervan Publishing House. All rights reserved.

Scripture marked (ICV) is taken from the *International Children's Bible, New Century
Version*, copyright ©1983, 1986, 1988 by Word Publishing, Dallas, Texas 75039.
Used by permission.

Edited by Liz Duckworth
Designed by Keith Sherrer

First printing, 2000
Printed in the United States of America
04 30 02 01 00   5 4 3 2 1

Library of Congress Cataloging-in-Publication Data
Steinhauser, Michele.
      You can do great things/Michele Steinhauser; illustrated by Yudthana Pongmee.
            p. cm.
      Summary: Simple rhyming text and Bible verses emphasize that each individual is a special
creation of God, designed for doing great things.
            ISBN 0-7814-3449-1
      1. Children—Religious life—Juvenile literature. 2. Self-esteem—Religious aspects—
Christianity—Juvenile literature. [1. Self-esteem—Religious aspects—Christianity.
      2. Christian life.] I. Pongmee, Yudthana, ill. II. Title.

BV4571.2.S734 2000
242'.62—dc21

99-087449

Enjoy special moments with your child reading and journaling throughout this book. At the end, you will find a place to record the great things your child has done and make plans for great things in the future. This book will become a treasured keepsake for a lifetime.

The first time we saw you,
we held you so tight.
We knew you were special
and oh, what a sight.

Your skin was so soft,
your hands were so small.
The look in your eyes
inspired us all.

GOD had done great things.

God did a great thing when He made

_____. Born: _____
(childs name)   (date)

"[You are] fearfully and wonderfully made."
Psalm 139:14a (NASB)

Great things God gave me:

"Stand and
consider
the wonders
of God."
Job 37:14b (NASB)

And as you grow older,
the more amazing you get.
You have lots of things
that are common and yet,
you're simply like nobody
else that we know.

So we want you to know
that wherever you go
in this great, great big world,
there's so much for you,
so much to see and so much to do.
And we're always, in all ways,
believing in you.

God made YOU for great things.

Enjoy a bright flower's fragrance,
  or the deepest pine wood,
  and bread that is baking
  then tasting so good.

Freshly cut grasses
  and ripe apple trees,
  crackling campfires,
  and new fallen leaves:

You can **SMELL** great things

Great things I can smell…

"Through his power all things were made … things seen and unseen." Colossians 1:16a (ICV)

You can SEE great things.

"Your word is a lamp to my feet and a light for my path." Psalm 119:105 (NIV)

Watch the moon and the stars
giving light to the sky;
stare upward in awe
while watching geese fly.

White falling snow
with crystalline flakes,
cold frosted trees,
and iced-over lakes:

Great things I can see:

Great things I can hear:

WHOO!

You

"Behold, I stand at the door and knock; if anyone hears My voice and opens the door, I will come in to him." Revelation 3:20 (NASB)

An owl whoo-whoo-ing
on dark summer nights,
perched high in a tree
and so out of sight,

A cricket crick-cricking,
a bee that goes buzzzzz,
you know that they're there
and all just because:

can HEAR great things.

Great things I can hold:

"Examine everything carefully; hold fast to that which is good."
1 Thessalonians 5:21 (NASB)

Reach for small creepy spiders,
and soft puppy dogs,
warm clay and hard rocks,
and some wet pollywogs.

You'll find colorful shells
peeking out of the sand,
and oh, how I love
when you're taking my hand.

You can HOLD great things.

Feel the wind in your hair
and the sun on your face,
the sand through your fingers,
a loving embrace,

A tug in your heart,
or a tear from your eye,
then laughing so hard
that you really do cry.

You can FEEL great things.

Great things I can feel:

"A joyful heart is good medicine."
Proverbs 17:22a (NASB)

Great things I can be...

You can PURSUE

You're unique,
your own person,
distinctively you,

You're quite special,
important,
magnificent too!

And oh, how we're always
believing in you.

great things.

"Commit your works to the Lord and your plans will be established."

Proverbs 16:3 (NASB)

You can build castles
    or cities or towns,
    or choose to be funny
    like actors or clowns;
    you can help people
    by making them well,
    or bake lovely pastries,
    or find things to sell.

You can say "please" and "thank you."
    "You're special." "You're nice."
    "I'm sorry." "You're welcome."
    "You're sweeter than spice."
    "I love you." "I miss you."
    "I hope you'll come twice!"

P.S. Jesus loves you
    (and paid a great price).

These are some real

Great things I can say:

My great things!

"Therefore encourage one another and build each other up." 1 Thessalonians 5:11 (NIV)

You can lead others to places so high.
You can paint rainbows as colors go by.
You can make music reach up to the sky.

And if you aim high
   where the eagles do soar,
   you can be what you want
   and do anything more.

You can DREAM great things.

Great things I can dream:

"Those who wait for the Lord will gain new strength; they will mount up with wings like eagles, they will run and not get tired.

Isaiah 40:31 (NASB)

And if anyone tells you,
"You can't do it. Oh my!
That's much, much too far
or that's much, much too high,"
or they say you're too short,
or they say you're too tall,
or you're much, much too big,
or you're simply too small,

Or that doesn't smell good,
or that doesn't look nice,
or that doesn't feel warm,
or that's too high a price,

Great things I can try:

Or you mustn't think that,
    it will take much too long,
    you can't dream such a thing,
    you can't sing such a song.

Just look at them, and smile,
    and give a little Oh-sigh,
    because if you think that you can,
    you can certainly try!

Great things I treasure in my heart:

For great is not measured
by how large or how much,
or by trophies or money,
or stardom or such,

But the greatest of things
are by whole or in part,
measured by how they affect
each one's heart.

"For where your treasure is, there will your heart be also." Matthew 6:21 (NASB)

So seek to show love,
    with peace on your mind.
    Be patient and good,
    and strive to be kind,

Try to be thoughtful and gentle each day
    have self-control, faith,
    and joy on your way.

Great things God wants to see in me:

The fruit of the Spirit is love, joy, peace, patience, kindness, goodness, faithfulness, gentleness, self-control; against such things there is no law.
Galatians 5:22, 23 (NASB)

Whatever you find
in this world to do,
whatever is good
and whatever is true,
God has a marvelous plan just for you.

You can DO great things.

Great things God wants to do through me:

...of day. Proverbs 4:18 (NIV)

On top of how great you are, just being you, here are some great things that we've seen you do!

Date   **Great thing you did**

_____   _____

_____   _____

_____   _____

_____   _____

_____   _____

_____   _____

_____   _____

_____   _____

_____   _____

_____   _____

_____   _____

_____   _____

_____   _____

_____   _____

On top of all that you are and all that you'll be, here are some great things you've said that we'll see!

Date	Great thing you'll do
_____	_____
_____	_____
_____	_____
_____	_____
_____	_____
_____	_____
_____	_____
_____	_____
_____	_____
_____	_____
_____	_____
_____	_____
_____	_____
_____	_____

You Can Do Great Things

Ages: 4-7

Life Issue: My child needs to understand that
God has created each of us for a unique purpose.

Spiritual Building Block: Love/Confidence

Learning Styles

Sight: While your child is looking in a mirror, talk about special physical features that make your child unique. Study together hair color and texture, eye shape and hue, that special smile (with missing teeth?), length of fingers, height, shape of toes. Talk about ways God has made your child special inside, too. Discuss his or her kind heart, creative abilities, friendliness, love for animals, and other positive characteristics. Pray together, thanking God for making your child special.

Sound: Give your child an oral quiz, with him or her as the subject! Ask questions like: What's your favorite toy? What do you most like to do? Who is your best friend? What do you want to be when you grow up? What makes you sad? What makes you happy? Explain that nobody else would give the same answers, because God has made each one of us different and special. Memorize together Psalm 139:14, "You are fearfully and wonderfully made."

Touch: Experience together some of the "great things" God has given us to smell, see, hear, hold, and touch, by going on a nature walk outdoors. Count all the things you can discover through the senses. Listen to birds singing or crickets chirping. Smell flowers or musty leaves. Count all the colors you can find in the sky, on the ground, and in the growing plants all around. Hold hands. Then pray together, thanking God for His wonderful creation, and for giving us the ability to enjoy it.